Dear Tutor,

Here are some guidelines how to u

- The planner consists of two sections: the student's logs & lesson planner

The student's name:		Contact details:		
Grade / Level:				
The purpose of learning:				
The rate:		The length of the lesson:		
Week:	✓	Topic:	Plan:	Reading list:
Week 1				

- Section 1 allows you to write down all the necessary details regarding your student or the group such as the name, level, contact details, the length of the lesson, the rate / pricing and the purpose of learning. These details will always remind you what the student's goals are, and you will never forget about the plans, ideas and the topic of the lesson.
- You can make sure that you are prepared for the lesson by marking the 'checked box.'
- As for the topic, always write down as many details as possible, especially if the lesson is customized.
- Plan helps you to write down the ideas you have for the following lesson or write down what areas are problematic for the student.
- The reading list is dedicated to teacher's and learner's who lend / borrow the books, audiobooks, and any

other material. You will know exactly what article the student has read and never make a mistake to lend or print the same handout twice!

- You can use sticky index or bookmarks to find the student faster.

	Financials		
Week:	Earned:	Overdue Payments:	Monthly Totals:
Week 1			
Week 2			
Week 3			

- Section 2 is dedicated to private tutors, who have different terms and conditions with their students.
- You can write down how much you have earned and follow overdue payments. There is enough space to detail the payments. You can also use the check box in the weekly plan to confirm that the student has paid.

'The mediocre teacher tells.

The good teacher explains.

The superior teaches demonstrates.

The great teacher inspires.'

William Artur Ward

The best teacher uses a planner!

The student's name: .... Contact details: ....

Grade / Level: ....

The purpose of learning: ....

The rate: .... The length of the lesson: ....

Week:	✓	Topic:	Plan:	Reading list:
Week 1				
Week 2				
Week 3				
Week 4				
Week 5				
Week 6				
Week 7				
Week 8				
Week 9				
Week 10				
Week 11				
Week 12				
Week 13				
Week 14				

Week 15			
Week 16			
Week 17			
Week 18			
Week 19			
Week 20			
Week 21			
Week 22			
Week 23			
Week 24			
Week 25			
Week 26			
Week 27			
Week 28			
Week 29			
Week 30			
Week 31			

Week 32			
Week 33			
Week 34			
Week 35			
Week 36			
Week 37			
Week 38			
Week 39			
Week 40			
Week 41			
Week 42			
Week 43			
Week 44			
Week 45			
Week 46			
Week 47			
Week 48			

Week 49				
Week 50				
Week 51				
Week 52				
Week 53				

Remarks: ....
....
....
....
....
....
....
....
....
....
....
....
....
....
....
....
....
....

The student's name:		Contact details:		

The student's name: ....   Contact details: ....

Grade / Level: ....

The purpose of learning: ....

The rate: ....   The length of the lesson: ....

Week:	✓	Topic:	Plan:	Reading list:
Week 1				
Week 2				
Week 3				
Week 4				
Week 5				
Week 6				
Week 7				
Week 8				
Week 9				
Week 10				
Week 11				
Week 12				
Week 13				

Week 14			
Week 15			
Week 16			
Week 17			
Week 18			
Week 19			
Week 20			
Week 21			
Week 22			
Week 23			
Week 24			
Week 25			
Week 26			
Week 27			
Week 28			
Week 29			
Week 30			

Week 31			
Week 32			
Week 33			
Week 34			
Week 35			
Week 36			
Week 37			
Week 38			
Week 39			
Week 40			
Week 41			
Week 42			
Week 43			
Week 44			
Week 45			
Week 46			
Week 47			

Week 48				
Week 49				
Week 50				
Week 51				
Week 52				
Week 53				

Remarks: ....

....

....

....

....

....

....

....

....

....

....

....

....

....

The student's name:		Contact details:		
Grade / Level:				
The purpose of learning:				
The rate:		The length of the lesson:		
Week:	✓	Topic:	Plan:	Reading list:
Week 1				
Week 2				
Week 3				
Week 4				
Week 5				
Week 6				
Week 7				
Week 8				
Week 9				
Week 10				
Week 11				
Week 12				
Week 13				
Week 14				

Week 15			
Week 16			
Week 17			
Week 18			
Week 19			
Week 20			
Week 21			
Week 22			
Week 23			
Week 24			
Week 25			
Week 26			
Week 27			
Week 28			
Week 29			
Week 30			
Week 31			

Week 32			
Week 33			
Week 34			
Week 35			
Week 36			
Week 37			
Week 38			
Week 39			
Week 40			
Week 41			
Week 42			
Week 43			
Week 44			
Week 45			
Week 46			
Week 47			
Week 48			

Week 49			
Week 50			
Week 51			
Week 52			
Week 53			

Remarks: ....
....
....
....
....
....
....
....
....
....
....
....
....
....
....
....
....
....

The student's name: .... Contact details: ....

Grade / Level: ....

The purpose of learning: ....

The rate: .... The length of the lesson: ....

Week:	✓	Topic:	Plan:	Reading list:
Week 1				
Week 2				
Week 3				
Week 4				
Week 5				
Week 6				
Week 7				
Week 8				
Week 9				
Week 10				
Week 11				
Week 12				
Week 13				

Week 14			
Week 15			
Week 16			
Week 17			
Week 18			
Week 19			
Week 20			
Week 21			
Week 22			
Week 23			
Week 24			
Week 25			
Week 26			
Week 27			
Week 28			
Week 29			
Week 30			

Week 31			
Week 32			
Week 33			
Week 34			
Week 35			
Week 36			
Week 37			
Week 38			
Week 39			
Week 40			
Week 41			
Week 42			
Week 43			
Week 44			
Week 45			
Week 46			
Week 47			

Week 48			
Week 49			
Week 50			
Week 51			
Week 52			
Week 53			

Remarks: ....
....
....
....
....
....
....
....
....
....
....
....
....
....
....

The student's name: .... Contact details: ....

Grade / Level: ....

The purpose of learning: ....

The rate: .... The length of the lesson: ....

Week:	✔	Topic:	Plan:	Reading list:
Week 1				
Week 2				
Week 3				
Week 4				
Week 5				
Week 6				
Week 7				
Week 8				
Week 9				
Week 10				
Week 11				
Week 12				
Week 13				

Week 14				
Week 15				
Week 16				
Week 17				
Week 18				
Week 19				
Week 20				
Week 21				
Week 22				
Week 23				
Week 24				
Week 25				
Week 26				
Week 27				
Week 28				
Week 29				
Week 30				

Week 31			
Week 32			
Week 33			
Week 34			
Week 35			
Week 36			
Week 37			
Week 38			
Week 39			
Week 40			
Week 41			
Week 42			
Week 43			
Week 44			
Week 45			
Week 46			
Week 47			

Week 48			
Week 49			
Week 50			
Week 51			
Week 52			
Week 53			

Remarks: ....
....
....
....
....
....
....
....
....
....
....
....
....
....
....

The student's name:	Contact details: ....

The student's name: ....   Contact details: ....

Grade / Level: ....

The purpose of learning: ....

The rate: ....   The length of the lesson: ....

Week:	✔	Topic:	Plan:	Reading list:
Week 1				
Week 2				
Week 3				
Week 4				
Week 5				
Week 6				
Week 7				
Week 8				
Week 9				
Week 10				
Week 11				
Week 12				
Week 13				

Week 14				
Week 15				
Week 16				
Week 17				
Week 18				
Week 19				
Week 20				
Week 21				
Week 22				
Week 23				
Week 24				
Week 25				
Week 26				
Week 27				
Week 28				
Week 29				
Week 30				

Week 31			
Week 32			
Week 33			
Week 34			
Week 35			
Week 36			
Week 37			
Week 38			
Week 39			
Week 40			
Week 41			
Week 42			
Week 43			
Week 44			
Week 45			
Week 46			
Week 47			

Week 48			
Week 49			
Week 50			
Week 51			
Week 52			
Week 53			

Remarks: ....
....
....
....
....
....
....
....
....
....
....
....
....
....
....

The student's name: .... Contact details: ....

Grade / Level: ....

The purpose of learning: ....

The rate: .... The length of the lesson: ....

Week:	✓	Topic:	Plan:	Reading list:
Week 1				
Week 2				
Week 3				
Week 4				
Week 5				
Week 6				
Week 7				
Week 8				
Week 9				
Week 10				
Week 11				
Week 12				
Week 13				

Week 14			
Week 15			
Week 16			
Week 17			
Week 18			
Week 19			
Week 20			
Week 21			
Week 22			
Week 23			
Week 24			
Week 25			
Week 26			
Week 27			
Week 28			
Week 29			
Week 30			

Week 31			
Week 32			
Week 33			
Week 34			
Week 35			
Week 36			
Week 37			
Week 38			
Week 39			
Week 40			
Week 41			
Week 42			
Week 43			
Week 44			
Week 45			
Week 46			
Week 47			

Week 48				
Week 49				
Week 50				
Week 51				
Week 52				
Week 53				

Remarks: ....
....
....
....
....
....
....
....
....
....
....
....
....
....
....

The student's name: .... Contact details: ....

Grade / Level: ....

The purpose of learning: ....

The rate: .... The length of the lesson: ....

Week:	✓	Topic:	Plan:	Reading list:
Week 1				
Week 2				
Week 3				
Week 4				
Week 5				
Week 6				
Week 7				
Week 8				
Week 9				
Week 10				
Week 11				
Week 12				
Week 13				

Week 14			
Week 15			
Week 16			
Week 17			
Week 18			
Week 19			
Week 20			
Week 21			
Week 22			
Week 23			
Week 24			
Week 25			
Week 26			
Week 27			
Week 28			
Week 29			
Week 30			

Week 31			
Week 32			
Week 33			
Week 34			
Week 35			
Week 36			
Week 37			
Week 38			
Week 39			
Week 40			
Week 41			
Week 42			
Week 43			
Week 44			
Week 45			
Week 46			
Week 47			

Week 48			
Week 49			
Week 50			
Week 51			
Week 52			
Week 53			

Remarks: ....
....
....
....
....
....
....
....
....
....
....
....
....
....
....

The student's name:			Contact details:	

The student's name: .... Contact details: ....

Grade / Level: ....

The purpose of learning: ....

The rate: .... The length of the lesson: ....

Week:	✓	Topic:	Plan:	Reading list:
Week 1				
Week 2				
Week 3				
Week 4				
Week 5				
Week 6				
Week 7				
Week 8				
Week 9				
Week 10				
Week 11				
Week 12				
Week 13				

Week 14			
Week 15			
Week 16			
Week 17			
Week 18			
Week 19			
Week 20			
Week 21			
Week 22			
Week 23			
Week 24			
Week 25			
Week 26			
Week 27			
Week 28			
Week 29			
Week 30			

Week 31			
Week 32			
Week 33			
Week 34			
Week 35			
Week 36			
Week 37			
Week 38			
Week 39			
Week 40			
Week 41			
Week 42			
Week 43			
Week 44			
Week 45			
Week 46			
Week 47			

Week 48			
Week 49			
Week 50			
Week 51			
Week 52			
Week 53			

Remarks:
....
....
....
....
....
....
....
....
....
....
....
....
....
....
....

The student's name: .... Contact details: ....

Grade / Level: ....

The purpose of learning: ....

The rate: .... The length of the lesson: ....

Week:	✓	Topic:	Plan:	Reading list:
Week 1				
Week 2				
Week 3				
Week 4				
Week 5				
Week 6				
Week 7				
Week 8				
Week 9				
Week 10				
Week 11				
Week 12				
Week 13				

Week 14			
Week 15			
Week 16			
Week 17			
Week 18			
Week 19			
Week 20			
Week 21			
Week 22			
Week 23			
Week 24			
Week 25			
Week 26			
Week 27			
Week 28			
Week 29			
Week 30			

Week 31			
Week 32			
Week 33			
Week 34			
Week 35			
Week 36			
Week 37			
Week 38			
Week 39			
Week 40			
Week 41			
Week 42			
Week 43			
Week 44			
Week 45			
Week 46			
Week 47			

Week 48			
Week 49			
Week 50			
Week 51			
Week 52			
Week 53			

Remarks: ....
....
....
....
....
....
....
....
....
....
....
....
....
....
....

The student's name: .... Contact details: ....

Grade / Level: ....

The purpose of learning: ....

The rate: .... The length of the lesson: ....

Week:	✓	Topic:	Plan:	Reading list:
Week 1				
Week 2				
Week 3				
Week 4				
Week 5				
Week 6				
Week 7				
Week 8				
Week 9				
Week 10				
Week 11				
Week 12				
Week 13				

Week 14				
Week 15				
Week 16				
Week 17				
Week 18				
Week 19				
Week 20				
Week 21				
Week 22				
Week 23				
Week 24				
Week 25				
Week 26				
Week 27				
Week 28				
Week 29				
Week 30				

Week 31				
Week 32				
Week 33				
Week 34				
Week 35				
Week 36				
Week 37				
Week 38				
Week 39				
Week 40				
Week 41				
Week 42				
Week 43				
Week 44				
Week 45				
Week 46				
Week 47				

Week 48				
Week 49				
Week 50				
Week 51				
Week 52				
Week 53				

Remarks: ....
....
....
....
....
....
....
....
....
....
....
....
....
....
....
....

Week:	✓	Topic:	Plan:	Reading list:
Week 1				
Week 2				
Week 3				
Week 4				
Week 5				
Week 6				
Week 7				
Week 8				
Week 9				
Week 10				
Week 11				
Week 12				
Week 13				

The student's name: .... Contact details: ....

Grade / Level: ....

The purpose of learning: ....

The rate: .... The length of the lesson: ....

Week 14			
Week 15			
Week 16			
Week 17			
Week 18			
Week 19			
Week 20			
Week 21			
Week 22			
Week 23			
Week 24			
Week 25			
Week 26			
Week 27			
Week 28			
Week 29			
Week 30			

Week 31			
Week 32			
Week 33			
Week 34			
Week 35			
Week 36			
Week 37			
Week 38			
Week 39			
Week 40			
Week 41			
Week 42			
Week 43			
Week 44			
Week 45			
Week 46			
Week 47			

Week 48				
Week 49				
Week 50				
Week 51				
Week 52				
Week 53				

Remarks: ....
....
....
....
....
....
....
....
....
....
....
....
....
....
....

The student's name:	Contact details: ....

The purpose of learning: ....

Grade / Level: ....

The rate: ....   The length of the lesson: ....

Week:	✓	Topic:	Plan:	Reading list:
Week 1				
Week 2				
Week 3				
Week 4				
Week 5				
Week 6				
Week 7				
Week 8				
Week 9				
Week 10				
Week 11				
Week 12				
Week 13				

Week 14			
Week 15			
Week 16			
Week 17			
Week 18			
Week 19			
Week 20			
Week 21			
Week 22			
Week 23			
Week 24			
Week 25			
Week 26			
Week 27			
Week 28			
Week 29			
Week 30			

Week 31			
Week 32			
Week 33			
Week 34			
Week 35			
Week 36			
Week 37			
Week 38			
Week 39			
Week 40			
Week 41			
Week 42			
Week 43			
Week 44			
Week 45			
Week 46			
Week 47			

Week 48			
Week 49			
Week 50			
Week 51			
Week 52			
Week 53			

Remarks: ....
....
....
....
....
....
....
....
....
....
....
....
....
....

The student's name: .... Contact details: ....

Grade / Level: ....

The purpose of learning: ....

The rate: .... The length of the lesson: ....

Week:	✔	Topic:	Plan:	Reading list:
Week 1				
Week 2				
Week 3				
Week 4				
Week 5				
Week 6				
Week 7				
Week 8				
Week 9				
Week 10				
Week 11				
Week 12				
Week 13				

Week 14			
Week 15			
Week 16			
Week 17			
Week 18			
Week 19			
Week 20			
Week 21			
Week 22			
Week 23			
Week 24			
Week 25			
Week 26			
Week 27			
Week 28			
Week 29			
Week 30			

Week 31			
Week 32			
Week 33			
Week 34			
Week 35			
Week 36			
Week 37			
Week 38			
Week 39			
Week 40			
Week 41			
Week 42			
Week 43			
Week 44			
Week 45			
Week 46			
Week 47			

Week 48				
Week 49				
Week 50				
Week 51				
Week 52				
Week 53				

Remarks: ....
....
....
....
....
....
....
....
....
....
....
....
....
....
....

The student's name:			Contact details:	

The student's name: .... Contact details: ....

Grade / Level: ....

The purpose of learning: ....

The rate: .... The length of the lesson: ....

Week:	✔	Topic:	Plan:	Reading list:
Week 1				
Week 2				
Week 3				
Week 4				
Week 5				
Week 6				
Week 7				
Week 8				
Week 9				
Week 10				
Week 11				
Week 12				
Week 13				

Week 14			
Week 15			
Week 16			
Week 17			
Week 18			
Week 19			
Week 20			
Week 21			
Week 22			
Week 23			
Week 24			
Week 25			
Week 26			
Week 27			
Week 28			
Week 29			
Week 30			

Week 31			
Week 32			
Week 33			
Week 34			
Week 35			
Week 36			
Week 37			
Week 38			
Week 39			
Week 40			
Week 41			
Week 42			
Week 43			
Week 44			
Week 45			
Week 46			
Week 47			

Week 48			
Week 49			
Week 50			
Week 51			
Week 52			
Week 53			

Remarks: ....

....

....

....

....

....

....

....

....

....

....

....

....

....

....

....

....

The student's name:	Contact details: ....

Grade / Level: ....

The purpose of learning: ....

The rate:	The length of the lesson: ....

Week:	✓	Topic:	Plan:	Reading list:
Week 1				
Week 2				
Week 3				
Week 4				
Week 5				
Week 6				
Week 7				
Week 8				
Week 9				
Week 10				
Week 11				
Week 12				
Week 13				

Week 14			
Week 15			
Week 16			
Week 17			
Week 18			
Week 19			
Week 20			
Week 21			
Week 22			
Week 23			
Week 24			
Week 25			
Week 26			
Week 27			
Week 28			
Week 29			
Week 30			

Week 31			
Week 32			
Week 33			
Week 34			
Week 35			
Week 36			
Week 37			
Week 38			
Week 39			
Week 40			
Week 41			
Week 42			
Week 43			
Week 44			
Week 45			
Week 46			
Week 47			

Week 48			
Week 49			
Week 50			
Week 51			
Week 52			
Week 53			

Remarks:

....

....

....

....

....

....

....

....

....

....

....

....

....

....

....

The student's name:		Contact details: ....

The student's name: .... Contact details: ....
Grade / Level: ....
The purpose of learning: ....
The rate: .... The length of the lesson: ....

Week:	✓	Topic:	Plan:	Reading list:
Week 1				
Week 2				
Week 3				
Week 4				
Week 5				
Week 6				
Week 7				
Week 8				
Week 9				
Week 10				
Week 11				
Week 12				
Week 13				

Week 14			
Week 15			
Week 16			
Week 17			
Week 18			
Week 19			
Week 20			
Week 21			
Week 22			
Week 23			
Week 24			
Week 25			
Week 26			
Week 27			
Week 28			
Week 29			
Week 30			

Week 31				
Week 32				
Week 33				
Week 34				
Week 35				
Week 36				
Week 37				
Week 38				
Week 39				
Week 40				
Week 41				
Week 42				
Week 43				
Week 44				
Week 45				
Week 46				
Week 47				

Week 48			
Week 49			
Week 50			
Week 51			
Week 52			
Week 53			

Remarks: ....

....

....

....

....

....

....

....

....

....

....

....

....

....

....

| The student's name: .... | Contact details: .... |

The student's name: .... Contact details: ....

Grade / Level: ....

The purpose of learning: ....

The rate: .... The length of the lesson: ....

Week:	✓	Topic:	Plan:	Reading list:
Week 1				
Week 2				
Week 3				
Week 4				
Week 5				
Week 6				
Week 7				
Week 8				
Week 9				
Week 10				
Week 11				
Week 12				
Week 13				

Week 14			
Week 15			
Week 16			
Week 17			
Week 18			
Week 19			
Week 20			
Week 21			
Week 22			
Week 23			
Week 24			
Week 25			
Week 26			
Week 27			
Week 28			
Week 29			
Week 30			

Week 31			
Week 32			
Week 33			
Week 34			
Week 35			
Week 36			
Week 37			
Week 38			
Week 39			
Week 40			
Week 41			
Week 42			
Week 43			
Week 44			
Week 45			
Week 46			
Week 47			

Week 48			
Week 49			
Week 50			
Week 51			
Week 52			
Week 53			

Remarks:

....
....
....
....
....
....
....
....
....
....
....
....
....
....
....

The student's name: .... Contact details: ....

Grade / Level: ....

The purpose of learning: ....

The rate: .... The length of the lesson: ....

Week:	✓	Topic:	Plan:	Reading list:
Week 1				
Week 2				
Week 3				
Week 4				
Week 5				
Week 6				
Week 7				
Week 8				
Week 9				
Week 10				
Week 11				
Week 12				
Week 13				

Week 14			
Week 15			
Week 16			
Week 17			
Week 18			
Week 19			
Week 20			
Week 21			
Week 22			
Week 23			
Week 24			
Week 25			
Week 26			
Week 27			
Week 28			
Week 29			
Week 30			

Week 31			
Week 32			
Week 33			
Week 34			
Week 35			
Week 36			
Week 37			
Week 38			
Week 39			
Week 40			
Week 41			
Week 42			
Week 43			
Week 44			
Week 45			
Week 46			
Week 47			

Week 48			
Week 49			
Week 50			
Week 51			
Week 52			
Week 53			

Remarks: ....
....
....
....
....
....
....
....
....
....
....
....
....
....

The student's name: .... Contact details: ....

Grade / Level: ....

The purpose of learning: ....

The rate: .... The length of the lesson: ....

Week:	✓	Topic:	Plan:	Reading list:
Week 1				
Week 2				
Week 3				
Week 4				
Week 5				
Week 6				
Week 7				
Week 8				
Week 9				
Week 10				
Week 11				
Week 12				
Week 13				

Week 14			
Week 15			
Week 16			
Week 17			
Week 18			
Week 19			
Week 20			
Week 21			
Week 22			
Week 23			
Week 24			
Week 25			
Week 26			
Week 27			
Week 28			
Week 29			
Week 30			

Week 31			
Week 32			
Week 33			
Week 34			
Week 35			
Week 36			
Week 37			
Week 38			
Week 39			
Week 40			
Week 41			
Week 42			
Week 43			
Week 44			
Week 45			
Week 46			
Week 47			

Week 48			
Week 49			
Week 50			
Week 51			
Week 52			
Week 53			

Remarks: ....

....

....

....

....

....

....

....

....

....

....

....

....

....

....

The student's name:		Contact details:		

Grade / Level: ....

The purpose of learning: ....

The rate:	The length of the lesson: ....

Week:	✓	Topic:	Plan:	Reading list:
Week 1				
Week 2				
Week 3				
Week 4				
Week 5				
Week 6				
Week 7				
Week 8				
Week 9				
Week 10				
Week 11				
Week 12				
Week 13				

Week 14			
Week 15			
Week 16			
Week 17			
Week 18			
Week 19			
Week 20			
Week 21			
Week 22			
Week 23			
Week 24			
Week 25			
Week 26			
Week 27			
Week 28			
Week 29			
Week 30			

Week 31			
Week 32			
Week 33			
Week 34			
Week 35			
Week 36			
Week 37			
Week 38			
Week 39			
Week 40			
Week 41			
Week 42			
Week 43			
Week 44			
Week 45			
Week 46			
Week 47			

Week 48			
Week 49			
Week 50			
Week 51			
Week 52			
Week 53			

Remarks: ....
....
....
....
....
....
....
....
....
....
....
....
....
....

The student's name:		Contact details:		
Grade / Level:				
The purpose of learning:				
The rate:		The length of the lesson:		
Week:	✓	Topic:	Plan:	Reading list:
Week 1				
Week 2				
Week 3				
Week 4				
Week 5				
Week 6				
Week 7				
Week 8				
Week 9				
Week 10				
Week 11				
Week 12				
Week 13				

Week 14			
Week 15			
Week 16			
Week 17			
Week 18			
Week 19			
Week 20			
Week 21			
Week 22			
Week 23			
Week 24			
Week 25			
Week 26			
Week 27			
Week 28			
Week 29			
Week 30			

Week 31			
Week 32			
Week 33			
Week 34			
Week 35			
Week 36			
Week 37			
Week 38			
Week 39			
Week 40			
Week 41			
Week 42			
Week 43			
Week 44			
Week 45			
Week 46			
Week 47			

Week 48				
Week 49				
Week 50				
Week 51				
Week 52				
Week 53				

Remarks: ....
....
....
....
....
....
....
....
....
....
....
....
....
....
....
....

The student's name:		Contact details:		
Grade / Level:				
The purpose of learning:				
The rate:		The length of the lesson:		
Week:	✓	Topic:	Plan:	Reading list:
Week 1				
Week 2				
Week 3				
Week 4				
Week 5				
Week 6				
Week 7				
Week 8				
Week 9				
Week 10				
Week 11				
Week 12				
Week 13				

Week 14			
Week 15			
Week 16			
Week 17			
Week 18			
Week 19			
Week 20			
Week 21			
Week 22			
Week 23			
Week 24			
Week 25			
Week 26			
Week 27			
Week 28			
Week 29			
Week 30			

Week 31			
Week 32			
Week 33			
Week 34			
Week 35			
Week 36			
Week 37			
Week 38			
Week 39			
Week 40			
Week 41			
Week 42			
Week 43			
Week 44			
Week 45			
Week 46			
Week 47			

Week 48				
Week 49				
Week 50				
Week 51				
Week 52				
Week 53				

Remarks: ....
....
....
....
....
....
....
....
....
....
....
....
....
....
....

The student's name: .... Contact details: ....

Grade / Level: ....

The purpose of learning: ....

The rate: .... The length of the lesson: ....

Week:	✓	Topic:	Plan:	Reading list:
Week 1				
Week 2				
Week 3				
Week 4				
Week 5				
Week 6				
Week 7				
Week 8				
Week 9				
Week 10				
Week 11				
Week 12				
Week 13				

Week 14			
Week 15			
Week 16			
Week 17			
Week 18			
Week 19			
Week 20			
Week 21			
Week 22			
Week 23			
Week 24			
Week 25			
Week 26			
Week 27			
Week 28			
Week 29			
Week 30			

Week 31			
Week 32			
Week 33			
Week 34			
Week 35			
Week 36			
Week 37			
Week 38			
Week 39			
Week 40			
Week 41			
Week 42			
Week 43			
Week 44			
Week 45			
Week 46			
Week 47			

Week 48			
Week 49			
Week 50			
Week 51			
Week 52			
Week 53			

Remarks: ....

....

....

....

....

....

....

....

....

....

....

....

....

....

....

The student's name:		Contact details:		
Grade / Level:				
The purpose of learning:				
The rate:		The length of the lesson:		

Week:	✓	Topic:	Plan:	Reading list:
Week 1				
Week 2				
Week 3				
Week 4				
Week 5				
Week 6				
Week 7				
Week 8				
Week 9				
Week 10				
Week 11				
Week 12				
Week 13				

Week 14			
Week 15			
Week 16			
Week 17			
Week 18			
Week 19			
Week 20			
Week 21			
Week 22			
Week 23			
Week 24			
Week 25			
Week 26			
Week 27			
Week 28			
Week 29			
Week 30			

Week 31			
Week 32			
Week 33			
Week 34			
Week 35			
Week 36			
Week 37			
Week 38			
Week 39			
Week 40			
Week 41			
Week 42			
Week 43			
Week 44			
Week 45			
Week 46			
Week 47			

Week 48			
Week 49			
Week 50			
Week 51			
Week 52			
Week 53			

Remarks: ....
....
....
....
....
....
....
....
....
....
....
....
....
....
....
....

The student's name: .... Contact details: ....

Grade / Level: ....

The purpose of learning: ....

The rate: .... The length of the lesson: ....

Week:	✓	Topic:	Plan:	Reading list:
Week 1				
Week 2				
Week 3				
Week 4				
Week 5				
Week 6				
Week 7				
Week 8				
Week 9				
Week 10				
Week 11				
Week 12				
Week 13				

Week 14			
Week 15			
Week 16			
Week 17			
Week 18			
Week 19			
Week 20			
Week 21			
Week 22			
Week 23			
Week 24			
Week 25			
Week 26			
Week 27			
Week 28			
Week 29			
Week 30			

Week 31			
Week 32			
Week 33			
Week 34			
Week 35			
Week 36			
Week 37			
Week 38			
Week 39			
Week 40			
Week 41			
Week 42			
Week 43			
Week 44			
Week 45			
Week 46			
Week 47			

Week 48			
Week 49			
Week 50			
Week 51			
Week 52			
Week 53			

Remarks: ....
....
....
....
....
....
....
....
....
....
....
....
....
....
....

The student's name: .... Contact details: ....

Grade / Level: ....

The purpose of learning: ....

The rate: .... The length of the lesson: ....

Week:	✓	Topic:	Plan:	Reading list:
Week 1				
Week 2				
Week 3				
Week 4				
Week 5				
Week 6				
Week 7				
Week 8				
Week 9				
Week 10				
Week 11				
Week 12				
Week 13				

Week 14			
Week 15			
Week 16			
Week 17			
Week 18			
Week 19			
Week 20			
Week 21			
Week 22			
Week 23			
Week 24			
Week 25			
Week 26			
Week 27			
Week 28			
Week 29			
Week 30			

Week 31				
Week 32				
Week 33				
Week 34				
Week 35				
Week 36				
Week 37				
Week 38				
Week 39				
Week 40				
Week 41				
Week 42				
Week 43				
Week 44				
Week 45				
Week 46				
Week 47				

Week 48				
Week 49				
Week 50				
Week 51				
Week 52				
Week 53				

Remarks: ....
....
....
....
....
....
....
....
....
....
....
....
....
....
....
....

The student's name: .... Contact details: ....

Grade / Level: ....

The purpose of learning: ....

The rate: .... The length of the lesson: ....

Week:	✓	Topic:	Plan:	Reading list:
Week 1				
Week 2				
Week 3				
Week 4				
Week 5				
Week 6				
Week 7				
Week 8				
Week 9				
Week 10	✓			
Week 11				
Week 12				
Week 13				

Week 14			
Week 15			
Week 16			
Week 17			
Week 18			
Week 19			
Week 20			
Week 21			
Week 22			
Week 23			
Week 24			
Week 25			
Week 26			
Week 27			
Week 28			
Week 29			
Week 30			

Week 31				
Week 32				
Week 33				
Week 34				
Week 35				
Week 36				
Week 37				
Week 38				
Week 39				
Week 40				
Week 41				
Week 42				
Week 43				
Week 44				
Week 45				
Week 46				
Week 47				

Week 48			
Week 49			
Week 50			
Week 51			
Week 52			
Week 53			

Remarks: ....
....
....
....
....
....
....
....
....
....
....
....
....
....
....
....

The student's name: .... Contact details: ....

Grade / Level: ....

The purpose of learning: ....

The rate: .... The length of the lesson: ....

Week:	✓	Topic:	Plan:	Reading list:
Week 1				
Week 2				
Week 3				
Week 4				
Week 5				
Week 6				
Week 7				
Week 8				
Week 9				
Week 10				
Week 11				
Week 12				
Week 13				

Week 14				
Week 15				
Week 16				
Week 17				
Week 18				
Week 19				
Week 20				
Week 21				
Week 22				
Week 23				
Week 24				
Week 25				
Week 26				
Week 27				
Week 28				
Week 29				
Week 30				

Week 31			
Week 32			
Week 33			
Week 34			
Week 35			
Week 36			
Week 37			
Week 38			
Week 39			
Week 40			
Week 41			
Week 42			
Week 43			
Week 44			
Week 45			
Week 46			
Week 47			

Week 48			
Week 49			
Week 50			
Week 51			
Week 52			
Week 53			

Remarks: ....
....
....
....
....
....
....
....
....
....
....
....
....
....
....
....

The student's name:	Contact details: ....

Grade / Level: ....

The purpose of learning: ....

| The rate: .... | The length of the lesson: .... |

Week:	✓	Topic:	Plan:	Reading list:
Week 1				
Week 2				
Week 3				
Week 4				
Week 5				
Week 6				
Week 7				
Week 8				
Week 9				
Week 10				
Week 11				
Week 12				
Week 13				

Week 14			
Week 15			
Week 16			
Week 17			
Week 18			
Week 19			
Week 20			
Week 21			
Week 22			
Week 23			
Week 24			
Week 25			
Week 26			
Week 27			
Week 28			
Week 29			
Week 30			

Week 31			
Week 32			
Week 33			
Week 34			
Week 35			
Week 36			
Week 37			
Week 38			
Week 39			
Week 40			
Week 41			
Week 42			
Week 43			
Week 44			
Week 45			
Week 46			
Week 47			

Week 48			
Week 49			
Week 50			
Week 51			
Week 52			
Week 53			

Remarks: ....

....

....

....

....

....

....

....

....

....

....

....

....

....

....

....

Week:	Financials		
	Earned:	Overdue Payments:	Monthly Totals:
Week 1			
Week 2			
Week 3			
Week 4			
Week 5			
Week 6			
Week 7			
Week 8			
Week 9			
Week 10			

Week 11			
Week 12			
Week 13			
Week 14			
Week 15			
Week 16			
Week 17			
Week 18			
Week 19			
Week 20			
Week 21			
Week 22			

Week 23			
Week 24			
Week 25			
Week 26			
Week 27			
Week 28			
Week 29			
Week 30			
Week 31			
Week 32			
Week 33			
Week 34			

Week 35			
Week 36			
Week 37			
Week 38			
Week 39			
Week 40			
Week 41			
Week 42			
Week 43			
Week 44			
Week 45			
Week 46			

Week 47			
Week 48			
Week 49			
Week 50			
Week 51			
Week 52			
Week 53			